Sacred Lotus

A NOVELLA

ANTWAN CARTER

ISBN: 978-1-09836-535-6 (print)
ISBN: 978-1-09836-536-3 (ebook)

ANTWAN CARTER

Sacred Lotus

Antwan Carter is an author of two poetry books: *Cartier's Rose* and *The Story of A Thousand Petals*. His books are insightful, innovative, and inspiring. He is writing not only to leave a legacy in life but to change his readers' perspectives. He was born and raised in Boston, Massachusetts.

You can find more about this author on his Facebook page Cartier Rose or follow him on Twitter @ CartierRose3

Praise for the Work of Antwan Carter

"Antwan Carter has written a remarkable group of poems in The Story of a Thousand Petals. These poems are a testament to the power of the human heart, and the brain and the spirit as well."

—Harvey A. Silverglate
Attorney, Activist and Author of **Three Felonies a Day** and
Conviction Machine

"I thought that the book was insightful and eye opening. I greatly enjoyed it and thought family tree was heartfelt and relatable."

—William Powers, Author of *Mea Culpa*

"Well this is a very humbling and opening experience. Through the author's words, one can sense the things this person could have went through in order to write from such depth. This collection bleeds life and replenishes a sense of hope."

—Dana Ruff,
Author

"Carter is an ambitious writer with an independent voice and original perspective. This collection of poems, haiku, acrostics, and prose, gives glimpses into a life complicated by hard lessons, incarceration, and isolation. Yet profound faith, vivid emotion, and sudden truths show up at unexpected moments. At times inspiring, at times nostalgic. "The Story of a Thousand Petals" is confident and real. Cleary inspired by writers such as Paulo Coelho and Maya Angelou. Carter experiments with incorporating their words and philosophies as well as searching for his own. Looking forward to more writing from this author!

—Molly Campbell
English Lecturer
University of New Hampshire

Also by Antwan Carter

Cartier's Rose: Each Petal Tells a Different Story

The Story of A Thousand Petals

FOREWORD

Antwan Carter originally contacted me via regular old paper - post, and what developed in the years after has been a semi- regular exchange of notes and books in which we've discussed writing, authors and inspiration. Often the constraints of my busy life would delay my side of the conversation, but Antwan applied a steady and serious dedication to writing practice, and I have found myself often surprised by the appearance of a complete text such as "The Sacred Lotus." Through a difficult year, with very few resources, Antwan has engaged in blending history, religion and mysticism into a unique story that explores how to pursue self-fulfillment and enlightenment. Part story, part instruction, part history, he has woven together some familiar names and faces in order to create a new fable.

Dedication and inspiration drove Antwan to produce this novella, containing a message of optimism and hope that he seeks to bring to the world. Without the benefit of money, editors or agents. Antwan continues to bring his own truth to the practice of writing, sharing it in order to inspire others. It has been wonderful seeing Antwan's work develop to the point of producing this work. Which he has referenced as his masterpiece, but I suspect that his journey and writing will continue to grow.

Molly Campbell
Senior Lecturer
University Of New Hampshire

For God, who keeps my heart beating...
For my Grandmothers, who watch over me as they sit in heaven...
And Life, for she inspires me every day as I encounter its mysteries...

"Consider the lilies of the field, how they grow they neither toil nor spin,and yet I say to you that even Solomon in all his glory was not arrayed like one of these"

Matthew 6:28-29

"What is a Flower?" A Question to the World

The beauty of a flower lies a
Mystery to us all
A receiver and giver of life, but
Yet its known to fall
How can something so important
Only come at a certain time?
A perfect example to us all but yet
We still cant seem to find
The balance between uniqueness and
The power that governs us all
What is a flower if you know then
Stand up tall!

Antwan Carter, *Cartier's Rose*

Beauty is present in all creation but the dangerous reality is that us humans are often cut off from that divine energy. Thus, allowing ourselves to be influenced by what other people think. In turn, denying our own beauty because others cant or wont recognize. Instead of accepting ourselves as we are, we try to imitate what we see around us. Not realizing little by little our soul fades, our will weakens, our confidence becomes diminished. And all the potential we had to make the world a more beautiful place withers away. We forget the maxim that once was told "The world is what we imagine it to be"

If you're curious, here's how we get it back...

There was a young teenage girl named Lami from the City of David, which is also known as Jerusalem, who wanted to know about the mysteries of life's creation. She believed that once discovered, it would decipher the algorithm to all things hidden. For a thousand years, her family tried through Sufism but each generation failed to unveil the secret mysteries of life. It appeared to her that the basic principles of Sufism have been lost from trial and error of each generation passing down the tradition but mixing it with different philosophies in hopes of discovering the soul of the universe. One generation incorporated Judaism, another incorporated Jainism, while another tried Daoism. Each tradition taught them something useful but true application got lost in interpretation.

Lami, true to her faith, continued seeking the truth solely by focusing on divine unity, which is to let go of the consciousness of other things until achieving constant consciousness of God. Called tarigat; The spiritual path or way towards God. "How do I become one with the divine energy of life's creation?" Lami thought to herself as she began walking the streets of Jerusalem. The more she thought about it, more thoughts began to emerge. "What if I never find the essence of life's creations?" A look of concern appeared on Lami's face as she began to think of herself becoming another failure in her line of ancestors. Despite the growing pains of growing up in the city of David there was a gnawing sense of urgency inside her heart to visit the Dead Sea. "All of your answers lie in the Dead Sea", she heard her spirit say to her.

Immediately she began walking the path in search of the way. Two miles had passed as she studied her surroundings. People of all ages conversing about Jerusalem, being the spiritual center to finding God, such as debates of old merchants on how many times Jerusalem had been captured. "People still arguing about the accuracy of historical events" Lami thought to herself

3

while smiling. Noticing a store that sold fresh fruits and bottled water, she stopped to refuel her energy.

The name of the store was Replenishments. Intrigued by its' name, Lami asked the store owner, "How did you come up with its name?" The owner smiled before answering, "I came up with the name from being a student of life." Lami responded, "Yeah tell me, what is a student of life?" The Owner explained, "A student of life is one who knows that there are certain principles in life that never change. Look at that bottle of water you're holding. The Earth needs it to sustain itself, your body needs it. Or take the bags of plums you're holding, it contains the necessary nutrients that will revitalize your mind, body, and soul for whatever journey travel".

"Interesting" Lami looked at him with intrigue.

"That's why it's called Replenishments, because every day we live, we are renewing life. You see?"

Lami quickly realized how powerful the owners words were. She took it as a sign that she was heading in the right direction. Exiting the store while walking, a raven crowed loud enough for Lami to notice its enchanting presence. It was soaring quite low in the sky as if looking for its next meal. Enraptured by its presence, Lami accidentally bumped into a woman dressed in regal colors. The robe was Jade, the exact color of her eyes.

"Are you lost my child?" "You seem not to know where you're headed." The mysterious woman said while gazing into Lami's eyes. Nervously, Lami smiled as she pointed to the raven soaring gracefully in the sky. "I see, but you haven't answered my question." Now Lami's attention was piqued by this strange woman who seemed so concerned about her. First she thought maybe it's one of the elders family members playing a game with her, then thought possibly a gypsy after some gold. "I am not lost, I am on a journey!" she exclaimed trying her best to appear confident. "We are all on journeys in life, what does yours consist of?"

"Something personal" stated Lami.

The woman responded, "In life, you never know who is sent to assist you on your journey. Ignorance and arrogance can rob you of your destiny."

Lami felt her stomach tighten as they gazed into each other's eyes for an awkward moment. She could sense that she knew this woman's purpose. Before confirming her intuition, the woman spoke again and this time it was clear. "I am in quest to find a girl who's been seeking to decipher the soul of the universe."

"And when you find the girl, how will you know?" Lami asked.

"Easy, I'm talking to her."

The mysterious woman began to explain to Lami that she is a pythia, traditionally known as an oracle. She started to break down the secrets of life's creation to those worthy of possessing its beauty. It has been written hundreds of years ago, long before I existed, that I would pass down the way of understanding of mother's creation to a wise young girl from the City of David. As they continued to walk, Lami began realizing she will soon possess the key to life's mysteries. "You ever observed a flower, its true purpose in nature?" the Oracle asked. Immediately, Lami thought it was some kind of test, so she decided to answer truthfully.

"I never really thought to deeply about it."

"It's the simplest things in life that teach us the most." The Oracle studied her face to see if her words were resonating. Confident that they were, she continued.

"My teacher Sophie taught me this by giving me a poem to study that was recovered from Ancient Egypt. It was written on a clay tablet in Byblos."

Lami knew from studying Greek mythology as a child that prophecies were given in poetry by oracles that had to be interpreted by students as well as priests. "What did it say?" Lami asked. The Oracle instructed Lami to grab a pen and a piece of paper to write this down because it would be important for her to remember in the future. The Oracle began reciting from memory the first lesson. Its rhythm had Lami thinking of an incantation. Not sure of its importance, eagerly she put the paper away to ensure she didn't miss anything as the Oracle continued speaking, "A flower is beautiful because it found its reason for living. Once you find your reason, you will find you purpose..." A few seconds passed by and the Oracle continued, "Why do you think flowers put so much energy into attracting bees? Because it longs for notoriety, and it's only satisfied when its beauty can be exalted. Outer beauty is inner beauty made visible, and it manifests itself in the light that flows from the sun." The Oracle could see she had Lami's full attention. "But even before this takes place, there's a much more important process." Intrigued, Lami asked, "What?"

"Its transformation. Transformations are what help us love the mystery. Without them, the flower cant grow into its true potential or purpose. Just like you."

Confused, Lami began to think that she must somehow transform herself in order to possess the key to life's creations. She began to ponder if this transformation would have to take place physically or mentally. Not sure, she asked the Oracle. The Oracle smiled before answering, "Everything in life goes from one stage to another. It's the cycle of life. If one doesn't, one withers away before ever reaching its true potential and purpose. For example, take a bird when it's in its first stage, an egg. The bird must somehow find its way out on its own free will. If the mother decides to help the bird, it doesn't develop the necessary strength to fend for itself. Basically, it loses out on the most important lesson that life has to teach it, which hinders it from reaching its full potential. To answer your question, one has to transform mentally and physically, but mostly mentally."

"How does it happen?"

"It happens through two things. One is through joy and the other is through enthusiasm." The Oracle could see the baffled look on Lami's face, probably thinking both are the same.

"Joy is one of the main blessings of the all-powerful. If we are happy, we are on the right road. Enthusiasm is the sacred fire that lives in every creations heart. When you follow what fills you with enthusiasm, it's a sign of respect for that mystery..."

Knowledge that was once outside of Lami's awareness became alive. As she listened, "Every creation in the universe has a dream in its heart. It's when you follow it, the transformation process begins." Lami nodded in silence understanding now what the Orcale meant.

"Just like you, you can't see the transformation happening, but it is. As long as you keep following your heart's dream, it will manifest itself."

The Oracle felt the importance of teaching Lami the needs for solitude. Just like love is important for life to perpetuate, solitude is the essential condition needed in finding ones destiny. The Oracle continued, "Yet without solitude, the natural joy of one's heart can't reach the heavens where transformations take place. No soil can remain productive, no flowers can survive. Solitude is not the exclusion of company, but the moment our soul is free to speak to us helping us decide what to do with our lives."

Absorbed in thought from the Oracle's teaching, Lami began to take in everything around her. Noticing the skies' prominent color that gradually changes as the day proceeded towards the night, reflecting a constant rebirth of a new sky with each passing day. Cloaked in awe, Lami's attention moved along to the wind. Lami wondered how its direct source of origin when it comes to blowing has never been known by mankind. There has to be a hand that evokes it to move in many different directions. Yet she knows from the Oracle's teaching that even the wind goes through a transformation. Wanting to know more from all the unanswered questions conjured from her mind, she asked the Oracle, "Tell me more so that I can understand clearly."

The Oracle gave her a knowing look because she could see the burning desire for enlightenment in Lami's eyes." Understand small things in life are also responsible for great changes. Look at the rain that drops from the sky, the raindrops are nutrients for all of nature's creation. Without it, life cannot be sustained or bloom in a productive way. Everything in life is connected, open up your eyes, and you will see."

"Open my eyes? They are open, what do you mean?

"I mean unifying your heart with your eyes. Once they become one it will allow you to see the soul in every creation."

A few miles into Lami's journey, the Oracle notices Lami becoming tired. At Mount Olives, they both agreed to find a place to rest and continue tomorrow on their journey. A tent was put up while the Oracle instructed Lami to gather enough branches to start a fire. As Lami went onto her assignment, the Oracle went to hunt for dinner. By the time the Oracle was back, she had a bag full of berries and a mallard. The Oracle began preparing dinner as Lami watched in silence... The Oracle decided to reflect on memories when she was a young girl in Athens purposely to take Lami's mind from any anxious thoughts she might be having. The Oracle knew the mind and body must be at peace in order for the soul to do its' job. She switched subjects.

"The pythian games of Delphi was something I adored with a passion. I can still remember the solo signers angelic voices singing their best to enchant the crowd. Athletes from all over Greece came to compete in the Olympic games in hopes of being the one crowned with the crown of Laurel. These were great times."

Lami sat in silence as her thoughts began to wander, she thought about her mother Isabella who she called Yuma. How proud she would be for her being the first in multiple generations to unlock the algorithm to all things hidden from the naked eye. The thought of it made her fantasize of being treated as a messiah. Removing her village from the binds of being cut off from the Divine Love of nature. The wealth and respect that would be acquired, and how her family would be much better off. Lami would be the spiritual teacher of Tarigat, ensuring that its tradition would be passed onto each generation. Gazing into the future, things appeared bright. Branches began crackling in the fire, drawing Lami's attention back to the Oracle speaking.

"Odysseus was a story my mother used to tell me as a little girl. After hearing the story so many times, the seed was planted in my heart that I must go on my own spiritual journey. Are you familiar with the story?" Lami went through her memory palace but couldn't draw up anything definitively.

"I heard the name before but that's about it."

The Oracle continued on "Odysseus spent about twenty years traveling home from the Trojan War. Within that travel, he has marvelous adventures where he learns a great deal about himself and the world. Thrilled by what he discovers, he descends to the underworld to talk to the dead."

Lami was puzzled by Odysseus descending to the underworld to talk to the dead. "What is there that the dead needs to know?" thought Lami. As far as she could see, the dead had no similarity with the living. The meal the Oracle prepared was filling. Lami liked the way the meat tasted with fresh berries. The Oracle could sense that Lami couldn't grasp what she was teaching her.

Sometimes it's better to leave the seed that's been planted to nature, allowing time to water it, eventually growing to life. The Oracle remembered this from her own experience. Quickly feeling the need to change the direction of the way things were headed, she asked, "Do you know about the true history of Jerusalem and when it lost its way?"

"I know that Jerusalem is where King David and his son Solomon came from."

"It's more than where King David and his son Solomon came from. Jerusalem is the spiritual center. Its where most important events took place from a historical stand point. All the prophets in the Old Testament mention Jerusalem, Jesus visited Jerusalem, and it's where prophet Muhammad took his last breath an ascended to heaven. King David conquered Jerusalem in 1,000 B.C. and made it to the Capital of Israel. His son built the first holy temple to honor God about forty years later. Over the next several hundred years, the city was conquered and ruled by many different factions. However, the most significant loss of precious history took place after the holy city of Jerusalem was invaded by the Babylonians in 586 B.C. A significant number of Jews were held captive for revolting to its city being destroyed. The first temple King Solomon built to honor God was completely obliterated. Every ancient artifact inside was taken and sold throughout the eastern hemisphere. The majority of its buyers didn't know the true value of these artifacts, and so it went through many passing of hands. The Babylonians ruler Nebuchadnezzar ruled over Jerusalem for fifty years."

"How does this relate to myself and my journey?" Lami asked with a hint of impatience.

"If you allow me to carry on, everything will make sense. Somethings you just don't learn overnight, it comes over time. Does something in nature grow in one night reflecting its created purpose?" Respect the process or you will miss out on what life has to offer you, which is much more." A knowing look appeared on the Oracle's face as she begun smiling at Lami. Immediately the message registered, and Lami took it as another lesson being taught to her on this journey."

"Respect the process" Lami repeated to herself as she waited for the Oracle to carry on.

"In due time, things will begin to make much more sense" the Oracle said as she pointed to the night sky. "Seventy years later, after the leadership of Nebuchadnezzar, a person named Pindar stumbled upon a clay tablet as he was walking down a dirt road in the City of Athens. Inscribed was a poem written in Byblos. Pindar was a student of lyric poetry from Ancient Greece. Pindar believed that expressing oneself poetically was far more superior to other mediums of expression. It was once said that when Pindar was a youth, he was stung by a bee in his mouth, and this was the reason he became a poet of honey-like verses. The way that Pindar actually saw it was that poetry was the way of connecting the mind to the things that seemed unconnected. Bridging the gap of the visible and invisible world. Pindar was far beyond fascinated with his new discovery. He went so far as memorizing everything that was written. Day and night Pindar would work diligently to uncover its true meaning. Suddenly, a eureka moment dwelled upon him, leading him to Delphi, where he brought his revelation to the Oracle. Thoroughly impressed, the Oracle found in Pindar a ready pupil. She began teaching him the way of the sacred lotus."

"The Sacred Lotus" Lami whispered to herself with wonderment. The name had an esoteric ring to it, a mystical aura. "The Sacred Lotus is the truest way of connecting with God. When you look back at history going as far back to dinosaur ages, before humans existed, you'll notice flowers always existed, as they are one of the oldest creations in the universe. A lot of people overlooked the fact when Jesus told the Gentiles to consider the lilies of the field: how they grow, how they neither toil nor spin. In effect, he was saying that each human inhabiting the Earth, there is the spirit of the sacred lotus. It represents eternity, purity, and divinity. Jesus was a teacher of the sacred lotus. When Jesus was crucified, he had five wounds. These five wounds became symbolic to the five petals from a rose. Even before Jesus arrived on Earth, the angel Gabriel appeared to Virgin Mary, telling her she would bear God's child. Inside his hand was a lily, illustrating that he also was a teacher of the sacred lotus. It is said that when the Buddha attained enlightenment, there was a raised platform called the Jewel promenade shrine. Legend has it that wherever he stepped, a lotus flower sprang to life. In Buddhism, a lotus symbolizes the most exalted state of man. Its head held high, and undefiled in the sun. His foot rooted in the world of experience. Everywhere around you, you can find believers in the sacred lotus. The key is to know where to look."

As the Oracle's words lingered in the air, she continued to teach Lami more. "Every person spiritually awakened must carry on the tradition of the sacred lotus. Passing it onto those who are worthy of its secrets. Once you possess that light, you now have a responsibility of protecting its teachings. If gotten in the wrong hands, it can and will be defiled, leading humanity astray. This is why passing it on to those who are worthy is important. You don't choose to follow the sacred lotus, it chooses you. That's how it works."

"How come?" Thinking out loud, Lami interjected.

"It ensures that humanity is taught the right way and not the wrong way. Take for instance society as a whole doesn't believe in simplicity, they cant understand the richness of it. They think that everything is more complex than spiritual teachers or masters of some discipline makes it seem."

Lami sat there in a profound state of contemplation. In all of her fourteen years of living, Lami learned many stories about Jesus Christ, but nothing like this. Greek mythology was familiar territory for her. She had learned about Pindar and the Pythia Games in eight grade but nothing about discovering a clay tablet written in Byblos. So many questions began to emerge. How is this connected to Jerusalem, the sacred lotus, and her journey? Lami's mind was overloaded with so much information that immediately, Lami fell into a deep sleep from exhaustion of the days' events.

The Oracle noticed Lami fast asleep. She decided to carry Lami to their tent and gently tucked her in. The Oracle knew the feeling that Lami was experiencing as a young girl in search of her destiny. It was exactly the same for her when Sophie found her wandering the city streets of Athens. Unlike Lami having the dream to find the keys to life's creations, she aspired to be like Socrates, becoming skilled at getting people to question their beliefs. Quickly, she developed a reputation of being a gadfly, questioning people up and down the city streets. Sophie used to watch her for weeks and could sense in her spirit that she had found the right student, and taught her the way of the sacred lotus and becoming an Oracle. The Oracle smiled at this memory as she found herself fast asleep as well.

Awakened from a loud noise, Lami began to panic. Several voices began speaking forcefully in Arabic, "What are you doing resting in Mount Olives? Don't you know this land is Sacred?" The three men sized up the Oracle but she knew the man in the middle was the leader. All of them were dressed in military uniforms. The leader asked, "Where are you coming from?" The Oracle flashed a quick smile while gazing into the man's eyes. "I come from the city of David. I'm only here because my younger sister needed rest as we continue traveling on our journey."

"Journey? What kind of journey can you two be on?" as the three men in disbelief erupted in laughter. The Oracle knew that this man's arrogance will serve as his weakness. Taking advantage of this, she smiled and played to this man's ego. "We are traveling to the Dead Sea." "The Dead Sea? There is nothing fascinating about the Dead Sea. Only thing you can expect to find is a ton of salt" the leader said.

Lami listened in silence, wondering if there would be any more potentially dangerous encounters. Lami could hear the leader instructing the other soldiers that it was time to go. Before leaving he explained to the Oracle that they were leery of travelers because most were seeking revenge, or seeking to trade and sell secrets to rival countries. Seconds later, the Oracle burst into the tent, telling her to pack her things, for it was time to move on. Once she gathered all of her things, Lami stepped out of the tent and waited for the Oracle.

Glancing upwards into the sky, Lami noticed a raven again, soaring gracefully in the sky as it crowed in arrival of the morning's sun. Could this be the same exact raven that caught my attention outside of replenishments, she thought to herself. Before she could investigate her thoughts further, the Oracle appeared.

"I see you have been studying Phoenix." Lami nodded while pondering its uncanny arrival.

"Phoenix has been with you since you started dreaming of your journey as a little girl." The statement has Lami taken aback and before she could register a reply, the Oracle continued, "The purpose of him is to hunt, lead, and protect seekers of the sacred lotus."

Amazed at this revelation, Lami asked, "How is Phoenix connected to the sacred lotus?"

"Isn't it obvious to you by now? Everything I've taught you clearly illustrates its connection."

Becoming frustrated with herself, Lami thought back to some of the things she learned. Immediately, a light bulb flashed insider her head. The story of Jesus teaching the Gentiles of the significance of a flower came to remembrance: how the significance of the sacred lotus is within every living being. Representing purity, eternity, and divinity. Noticing the subtle light of excitement in Lami's eyes, the Oracle continued, "Phoenix is connected in spirit, its energy is in direct contact with the Divine Creator. Basically, he is an instrument used by God as a sign or omen."

Lami realized that her journey didn't just consist of her, but the entire universe. Could this be the algorithm to the universe? Lami knew now that she must pay close attention to everything in the universe, for a sign must be in plain sight. "As you grow in faith and more accustomed to the teachings, you will pick up on the nature of the universe." The Oracles words had an alchemical touch.

Traveling along the dirt road, Lami's attention was transfixed on the Oracle. Growing up as a child, she dreaded long periods of silence. To Lami, it felt close to destruction. Recognizing that she was closer to her dream, her heart became heavy. It was as if it was saddened by its new responsibility. The tale of the last supper came to mind as she remembered how Jesus talked about his soul feeling very sorrowful. A dose of fear began to spring to life inside her mind. "Fear not my friend, your dream will bring you more joys than you could ever imagine" said the Oracle as she sensed Lami's doubt.

The Oracle began to explain to Lami that when you become closer to achieving your dream, the enemy will use moments of doubt to try to tempt you away from your created purpose. "Did you hear when the three soldiers talked about the Dead Sea as if it were useless?" The truth is that the Dead Sea has been a supplier of a wide variety of things: Egyptian mummification, fertilizers, and many others. The Oracle began explaining how faith is very important in life. Some philosophers called it the elixir of life, for it allows the invisible hand of God to work, bridging the gap between the invisible and visible world. Pedestrians call these signs miracles but followers of the sacred lotus call them the manifestation of God spoken from the language of faith. "Enjoy quiet moments for it will allow your soul to grow stronger in faith" the Oracle said. She knew that a vast world lies hidden in our soul waiting to be discovered. In other words, quiet times incorporated with Faith gives the angels room to talk with our soul. "Think about this for a moment Lami."

They continued traveling on the dirt road path. Within the distance, they could see the Judean Mountains as they are directly across the Dead Sea. They could see the trees glowing in radiance, as several pedestrians traveled about on their journeys.

"What is beauty?" asks the Oracle

"Beauty is what attracts onlookers with admiration."

"I agree, yet is beauty all the same?"

"I would like to think so. Beauty is beauty and ugly is ugly. To me it's a simple perspective."

Impressed by Lami's answer, the Oracle decided to continue probing deeper. "True but beauty doesn't exist in sameness but in difference. So how can it be the same?" Unhinged by this response, Lami thought of it as a trick question. Silence became her answer. Noticing the puzzled expression on Lami's face, the Oracle continued nurturing Lami. "All beings created under the sun are reflections of the miracle of creation. Therefore, how can beauty exist in sameness?" Perplexed by this statement, Lami found it difficult to grasp its meaning. "A flower opening up is a miracle of life sent from the heavens. Golden leaves in autumn are making a way for new leaves in the spring. Each are beautiful in its own way but its not created in sameness, instead in uniqueness."

Lami started viewing the Judean Mountains pondering her future. The more she thought about it, the more eager she became to fulfill her destiny, the savior of her historical city. Lami could remember so many stories Yuma used to tell her about the paradigm for nations to follow with its sacred wisdom.

Jesus not only walked these same dirt paths as you, but those who also found it in their soul to glorify God. Follow your heart and study your life lessons and you'll uncover the invisible hand of God and become a vessel for ensuring that wisdom gets passed along to the people. "A person grows with the greatness of their task." Immediately, Lami could hear Yuma's voice saying this to her as a child and Lami knew her task was massive.

Thinking of all of this, Lami's mind began to travel backwards in time to when she attended high school for the first time. She remembered all of the rich students from wealthy countries that carried themselves with an air of entitlement and believed that their wealth dictated their social status in life. This invoked disgust deep down in Lami's spirit. She thought of the ignorance of these spiritually dead people, how they settled in honoring the physical world, and were unmoved by the signs of where all life came.

Grinning to herself, the Oracle glanced over and noticed the glint in her eyes. Up ahead, there was a crowd of people: men, women and children covered the path along with their goats and sheep, all walking. "Have you noticed up ahead my child?" asked the Oracle. "These are true followers of the sacred lotus." Lami looked in amazement, "How can you tell?" "Easy, once you become of the sacred lotus, you are in contact with the spiritual realm."

The Oracle went on to explain how they carry themselves with dignity. They know the true value of a person comes from humbling yourself before your creator. Material wealth doesn't ensure your prosperity in the afterlife. Words began to flash in Lami's mind as she heard Yuma's voice again, "Jesus demonstrated to his disciples that the words he was speaking to them were spirit and life." Suddenly the distance between them closed as they were near the believers. "Tanwir!" The Oracle said while gesturing her hands in the form of a pyramid. Tanwir translates to enlightenment. Paying attention to this, a revelation was formed in Lami's mind. She knew that the pyramid in Egypt was where the clay tablet was found, thus given birth to enlightenment. Everything was falling into place as the Oracle exchanged something with one of the followers. A goat began to follow them as they continued traveling along the dirt path. Lami wondered why the Oracle purchased a goat.

Hundreds of feet up ahead, there were pedestrians traveling up and down the dirt path road. The temperature was at its zenith as several travelers drank water from their canteen, struggling to remain hydrated in the heat. Where there are fewer trees, oxygen flow is constricted, making it difficult to breathe. The Oracle thought of the time when she traveled through the Sahara desert in Africa to see the pyramids. She knew how hot the sun could get and quickly affect not only your body, but your mind. The dunes in the desert of the Sahara are the mother of many mirages for hopeful travelers. The physical exertion it takes to walk up or down one is torturous. However, through it all she learned something useful. Sophie taught her that each follower of the sacred lotus must travel once in their lifetime to the pyramids in Egypt. For going there allows one's soul to experience the connection with the foundation of the universe. In other words, "All of life's creation. Egypt is known to all historians as the birthplace for all civilization. The Egyptians built the longest lasting civilization in history, thriving for 2,000 years. They invented hieroglyphics to communicate with spirits in the invisible world. Egyptians called it words of God. Words have a magical relationship with the universe as what is said in the present transitions into the afterlife. Mainly, the reason why Egyptians wrote on tomb walls, coffins, and papyri to protect and nurture souls in the afterlife."

Phoenix crowed three times as he dove out of the sky onto Lami's shoulder. Startled by the unannounced arrival, she jumped back causing Phoenix to lift back into the air as well. "Calm down Lami!" The Oracle shouted while gesturing for Phoenix to come to her. The Oracle began explaining to Lami that danger is near and that they must take a detour to avoid trouble. Lami couldn't perceive how there was danger as when she looked at her surroundings there didn't appear to be any sign of it. The trees were glowing, making use of the sun's brilliance, travelers moved about, taking in the days' beautiful presence. Normally, when the atmosphere changed, you could feel it. Lami felt nothing.

Lami and the Oracle fled the dirt path road onto the perimeter of the Judean Hills. Initially, they planned on crossing through Bethany into the Judean desert, which would have saved them time and energy to get to the Dead Sea. However, as everything in life happens for a reason, especially when dealing with the way of the sacred lotus, the Oracle decided that they should wait in a secluded area as Phoenix assessed the danger. Phoenix was trained to communicate the best route to travel and what it sees. They found a place to wait behind an area of abandoned buildings covered by trees. "Luckily Phoenix intervened before we walked into peril" the Oracle said while gauging Lami's reaction. Lami didn't understand the risks of following the sacred lotus. Just as there is a great reward for uncovering the truth, there is a greater danger trying to stop one from reaching the truth. Those forces are negative, designed to stop one from attaining one's true nature, because once you do, there's another stronghold broken on a human soul.

"You must understand something my child. When you declare yourself as a follower of the sacred lotus, there will be opposing forces trying to stop you from reaching your destiny."

Lami appeared baffled by this revelation, unable to connect the relation from earlier events. "Everything is connected, haven't you seen it manifested?" Embarrassed to admit, Lami's facial expressions confirmed what the Oracle already knew. "The essence of the universe is governed by forces, traditionally known as energy. Other cultures, even esoteric cults, refer to them as vibrations or frequencies. For every force, there is an equivalent opposite. For example, there is good energy and bad energy. This is the most basic element in the universe that most humans fail to acknowledge."

The Oracle went on to show Lami how everything was connected. From the so called accidental encounter between them outside of the store Replenishments, artfully caused by the crow of Phoenix. These were actual signs sent to you from the heavens of the sacred lotus. How about the three soldiers that arrived at our tents inquiring about our intentions. This was the equivalent force that used its servants to derail our journey. The Oracle explained how they outwitted them there but best believe they will be back.

"Do you think it was a coincidence that Phoenix dove out of the sky to warn us?" The Oracle said.

"At first I did, but now that you explained it to me I can see the connection."

"Lami, you must train yourself to grasp these signs. We avoid danger and overcome evil forces by staying attune with the universe."

Phoenix soared the horizons meticulously collecting information on where the sudden danger lay. Phoenix noticed soldiers quickly emerging from the Judean desert toward the direction of Bethany. They traveled on horses with their weapons brandished. You could sense that they were out for blood. Understanding this situation, Phoenix crowed while darting through the sky into the area of abandoned buildings where Lami and the Oracle hid. The Oracle made a gesture with her eyes and Phoenix gracefully flew onto her shoulder. The Oracle said something that sounded like tongues than any recognizable language. Phoenix began speaking back to the Oracle. After relaying the information, Phoenix flew over to Lami's shoulder "relax" the Oracle stated. "He is your helper you must treat him with love. Why don't you start by feeding him one of those berries you have inside your bag?" Lami did what she was told and Phoenix devoured it. Sensing how quickly he ate it, Lami gave him a couple more knowing he must by hungry. After eating, Phoenix rubbed his head on the center of Lami's neck. "He loves you Lami, he's showing you how to bond with him."

The more Lami begins to bond with Phoenix, the more Phoenix will reveal. Just as in the book of Job when he declares to his friend the mysteries of God. "Ask the animals and they will teach you, or the birds in the sky and they will tell you."

Now that the Oracle knows the soldiers are coming, they must move quickly for it's only a matter of time before they find them. Thinking about this, the Oracle's mind travels back in time when she was taught by Sophie that the followers of the sacred lotus have been hunted for thousands of years. When captured, they face endless torture such as beheadings, stonings, and public hangings.

"The soldiers are coming, we must figure out our next move" the Oracle said. "Where are they?"

"Traveling from the Judean desert towards Bethany by horses."

"Since we are at the perimeter of the Judean Hills, why not go inside and find a place to hide?"

"You know what? That's a good idea."

They began moving into the Judean Hills looking for a place to hide. The Oracle knew the best way to hide is in plain sight. People have a tendency to overlook what's right in front of them. It took them a couple of minutes to find the perfect place to blend in. They picked a wooded area surrounded by farm animals. If trouble came, they could use their goat to cause a disturbance with the other animals. Several hours went by inducing Lami to believe the coast was clear. As soon as she went to make a move, the Oracle yanked her back down. Immediately after, they could hear several footsteps and the heavy breathing of several horses. "They have to be close, they are traveling by feet" One of the soldiers said in Arabic. Several of the soldiers spread out throughout the wooded area. One decided to harass the animals by throwing rocks at them. Struck directly in the midsection was a baby calf, pandemonium ensued. Sheep, cows, and pigs scattered while yelling at top volume. "How do you expect us to find them by creating such a disturbance?" The eldest soldier said as he struck the young soldier for his stupidity. Lami became anxious causing her to move a degree above subtlety. The Oracle grabbed her indicating with her eyes to remain still. "Hey what was that?" One of the soldiers said pointing towards the direction of where Lami and the Oracle were hiding. Before the soldier could act on his intuition, Phoenix pierced the skies at top speed at the soldiers face. Total oblivion on his behalf, Phoenix dug his claws into his eyes causing him to scream in agony. Phoenix flew away as fast as he came. Two of the soldiers grabbed their wounded friend and assessed the damage. Realizing quickly that he would be blind for the rest of his life, they decided to end their search.

"You are being taught the mysteries of signs and omens which are the sacred power of the universe" the Oracle said to Lami as they began to continue their journey. There is a secret advantage Lami has but it will take time for her to fully realize. It takes growth through experience and application to reach that ultimate state. Once reached, literally all the things of the universe will be at her command. Back in ancient times, the city of David was known for its spiritual connection to the universe. Things of the universe were used to perform these miracles. Stars become a source not only of direction but of ethereal communication. Plants become a conduit to strengthen the spirit from harmful spirits. The father of wind stirred the seven seas to awaken humanity from its foolish practice. Everything that's around them could easily be made to fit a purpose.

"What a close call that was!" Said Lami while following the Oracle's every step throughout the wooded forest inside the Judean Hills. "Phoenix gouged that soldier's eyes right out" continued Lami. Silence enclosed them as they stepped on branches that were taken from trees. Lami didn't have a clue as to where they were headed. From what she could tell, they were going deeper into the Judean Hills instead of going back to where they left off. Judean desert was the quickest route to the Dead Sea. "Why aren't you speaking?" The Oracle thought for a moment before finally answering Lami. "You are experiencing things at a rapid pace. Yet you still lack the wisdom to clearly understand every lesson." The Oracle looked deeply into her eyes while speaking. "What do you mean by that?" A look of uncertainty covered Lami's face as she waited for answers.

"Phoenix risking his life for you so early before being initiated through the rites of passage in way of the sacred lotus. Phoenix has to teach you the foundation of using yourself to conspire with the universe is what I mean."

Dumbfounded by everything going on, Lami waited for the Oracle to continue on. She knew from experience the Oracle doesn't stop talking until her point is made. "This can only mean one thing. You are selected for an even greater purpose." The Oracle began to look out ahead of the trees pondering on how to reveal this ancient legend to Lami. Thousands of years ago when the all-powerful decided to give his descendants the key to realign all his descendants with their created purpose, he knew there would come a point in time when opposing forces met. The encounter would be so disruptive, that only one would reign victorious. Before choosing the person best suitable for this assignment, he began training his descendants through many examples. He taught them understanding in all things: from literature, wisdom, to language of the universe. As these teachings began passing down through hundreds of generations, it was preparing someone special for the future. Prophecies were declared that it would be a person after the universe's heart. Directly from birth, there would be an engraved symbol in Arabic meaning chosen in the center of their palm's lines. That's the one who will fight for the spirit of the universe when it arrives.

The Oracle's mind drifted back into the present from her most cherished memory. "Can I see your hands?" A look of bewilderment appeared on Lami's face. Irritated by Lami's response, the Oracle grabbed her hands and began studying them and deeply engraved in her palms "chosen". Now she knew there was no time to waste but to give her everything. "Lami, there is an ancient legend that every follower of the sacred lotus is told after being initiated. Thousands of years long before us, the all-powerful decided to give his creations the key to realign with their created purpose. He knew that there would come a time where opposing forces would meet and battle. One symbolized harmony and purity, and the other symbolized death, destruction, and absolute evil. He knew he had to create a person that would be strong enough to fight for the spirt of the universe. All of the teachings for several thousands of years throughout each generation, someone special would be born inside their spirit with all the teachings that would be reawakened on their journey." Stunned by this bombshell revelation, Lami stood speechless. "It makes perfect sense now why Phoenix risked his life for you."

The sacred lotus needs someone to teach people the basic principles of the oracles of God again. The Oracle knew that she had a heavy obligation to ensure that Lami learned the right way for whats at stake. Never in a million years did she see herself being the bridge for the sacred lotus. She knew of the legend, in fact, the story was told to her thousands of times. `Someone who is chosen will be tested for all humanity' lingered in her mind for as long as she could remember. Pulling herself out of that trance, the Oracle decided now was the best time to revisit why Odysseus went to the underworld to talk to the dead, teaching Lami its' significance. "Death is nothing but a door way to new life. So when I told you the story about Odysseus communicating with the dead, it was to show you the connection between all things: from visible to invisible, from positive to negative, from basic to difficult. It all has its beginning with the transference of its opposite energy. Hence, in Ancient Egypt, a saying was birthed, "We live today, we shall live again in many forms, we shall return." Lami took in everything and pondered this lesson. "Do you understand its importance?" asked the Oracle. "Death is the counterpart to life, in other words, the beginning to the end, the ying to the yang."

"Exactly! This is where the universe's source of true power comes from. Death is ignorant to this but life knows its' value. For how could life continue to procreate if there is no ending?"

Lami finally understood what the Oracle was teaching her all along. She knew that the true believer of the sacred lotus's purpose was to show death that she is not feared, but

embraced. For knowing her existence, it forces our soul to discover our created purpose before it's too late and becomes claimed by death.

"I got it!" Lami expressed with joy.

"What is it you got my child?" responded the Oracle with interest.

"I know the true meaning of being chosen and the created purpose of the sacred lotus."

"You do? Then tell me" a hint of doubt lingered behind the Oracle's words.

"Me being chosen is simple. My Yuma used to always tell me that being curious is your greatest gift. For it will make room for you, in life, bringing you one day before the great. All of my life, I've wondered what she actually meant. But now as I have begun searching for the secret to the universe, I realize it was in front of my face all along. I say this as once we realize that death isn't to be feared but embraced, it opens up a line of communication with our soul. This enables us to receive our gift from the heavens, and makes the world a more beautiful place. We all need to realize that the battle between good and evil no longer exists. It's merely the distortion of our minds trying to imitate others' gifts that causes destruction."

The Oracle smiled because she knew that Lami was ready now. The only thing left was reaching the Dead Sea to complete the rest of her journey. They continued walking through the Judean Hills as they noticed up ahead near Wadi Quilt a carrier. The Oracle instructed Lami to call Phoenix to her. As she did, Phoenix dove out of the sky gracefully landing directly on Lami's shoulder. Lami began feeding him some of the berries she had left over, remembering bonding is the key to becoming one with Phoenix. The Oracle taught Lami how to give Phoenix orders to follow. A look of disbelief appeared on Lami's face as if it couldn't be that simple. "Go ahead and try" the Oracle said while pointing at the carrier.

Lami did as she was told and immediately, Phoenix took off in direction of the carrier. They waited patiently for the carrier to reach them. While waiting, the Oracle wanted her pupil to know something important. "The spirit that flows through you is not your own, it's the sacred lotuses." Lami listened waiting for the Oracle to make her point. "You must follow the spirit of the sacred lotus for it will guide you to the light of the universe. Remember we travel through darkness to serve the light." A few minutes passed and the carrier arrived asking where they would like to travel. "To the Dead Sea" the Oracle told the carrier.

Finally, they arrive at the entrance of the Dead Sea. Lami began to marvel at the actual amount of sand before the Dead Sea. Immediately her heart started beating fast because she knew this was it: the place where her life changes forever. Paying attention to everything around her, she missed when the Oracle paid the carrier with a few pieces of silver. "One must be careful for quicksand pits. They are all around the Dead Sea" the Oracle says before grabbing the goat. "My child lets move closer to the sea and settle." After finding a perfect place to settle all of their belongings, the oracle held up one finger telling her to wait." Unsure of what was going on, Lami began to observe. What she saw was unlike anything she had imagined, but still, it made her wonder.

Lami could see the Oracle heading back to her. Something was in her hands, but she couldn't make out what it was until the Oracle came closer and dropped the branches from trees. The Oracle began making the symbol of the pyramid in the sand with some of the branches. While still kneeling down, the Oracle started a fire, igniting the branches that formed the pyramid. The smoke from the pyramid engulfed the sky as she instructed Lami to make the pyramid gesture while saying "Tanwir". Lami did what she was told and waited for what was to come next. "Did you memorize the poem I told you to write down at the beginning of your journey?" Lami nodded her head yes and the Oracle spoke again, "Recite it out loud penetrating the universe's soul." Lami closed her eyes visualizing each word inside her head and began to speak.

"The beauty of a flower lies a
Mystery to us all
A receiver and giver of life but yet,
Its known to fall
How can something so important only
Come at a certain time?
A perfect example to us all but yet we
Still cant seem to find
The balance between uniqueness and
The power that governs us all
What is a flower if you know than
Stand up tall!"

After Lami finished, the Oracle pulled out a sharp double edged knife and called the goat to her side. As soon as it came to her, the Oracle grabbed its neck swiftly slitting its throat. Lami watched in a state of confusion. The Oracle explained that back in Ancient times when demi gods and prophets walked the earth, they used goats as an offering to the universe's spirit, for its blood was potent. The Oracle then laid the body gently next to the burning pyramid. Smoke continued to rise into the air in shapes of miniature pyramids. The Oracle then proceeded to cut the tip of her index finger. Crimson red blood slowly exited the tip. The Oracle then passed the knife to Lami and she did the same. Lami watched her own blood drip from her finger. The Oracle grabbed Lami's hand and formed it together with hers. Together, they formed the symbol of the pyramid. The earth began to shake as the skies turned black, violent expressions of wind, thunder, and lightening roared. Penetrating the four corners of the earth, massive waves stirred from the waters of the Dead Sea. Lami watched everything unfold. From her right, she noticed sand storms springing to life, and to her left, Phoenix stood there with a piece of paper hanging from his mouth. Lami looked behind her and no sign of the Oracle appeared and this troubled her deeply. Lami decided to take the paper from Phoenix after motioning him to fly onto her shoulder. Written on it was a message from the Oracle.

"The balance of the world lies in your hands now Lami. You were chosen long before you existed. Everything you need to succeed, you possess. Remember always the spirit that flows through you is not your own, it's the sacred lotuses. And with this you must follow the spirit of the sacred lotus for it will guide you to the light of the universe. For we travel through darkness to serve the light!

Fair well my child,
The Oracle, Gabriella

A smile covered Lami's face because she finally knew the Oracle's name. Picking up her belongings, she headed into the storm knowing that there's work to be done. For the balance of the universe lies in her hands. She headed back home.

AUTHOR'S NOTE

When I set out to write this book, it was to show that we all carry in our hearts a dream. For some of us, it may be hidden from many years of disappointment. And for others, it's the lack of courage to follow that inner calling within their own heart that has led them to abandon their dreams. I used a flower to show how it's the simplest things that we often overlook that mean the most and to give us an example of how we should live our lives. For every day a flower lives, it follows its created purpose. Can we say the same? Follow your DREAMS!

Other Books Coming Soon by Antwan Carter

"Diary of a Prisoner"

"The Truth Behind Justice: An Autobiography"

ACKNOWLEDGEMENT

First I would like to thank Kurt Eichner for allowing me to use his services to do the necessary research into this book. Without it, I would not have been able to put this together the way I did. Special thanks to Chelsea Pilling for she not only took the time to read my book in its infantile stage but shaped my ideas even when she didn't realize it. Also to Nicholas Quimby, who drew the book cover, a true artist. It takes a special gift to take a concept and bring into a medium the way you did.